3/10

**THREE RIVERS
PUBLIC LIBRARY DISTRICT**
www.three-rivers-library.org
Channahon, IL 60410
815-467-6200

DEMCO

Mysterious Encounters

La Llorona: The Crying Woman

by Q. L. Pearce

KIDHAVEN PRESS
A part of Gale, Cengage Learning

GALE
CENGAGE Learning

Detroit • New York • San Francisco • New Haven, Conn • Waterville, Maine • London

LIBRARY OF CONGRESS CATALOGING-IN-PUBLICATION DATA

Pearce, Q. L. (Querida Lee)
  La Llorona : the crying woman / by Q.L. Pearce.
    p. cm. -- (Mysterious encounters)
  Includes bibliographical references and index.
  ISBN 978-0-7377-4571-9 (hardcover)
  1. Llorona (Legendary character)--Juvenile literature. 2. Legends--Latin America--Juvenile literature. I. Title. II. Title: Llorona.
  GR114.P43 2010
  398.2098--dc22

                                                              2009028942

KidHaven Press
27500 Drake Rd.
Farmington Hills, MI 48331

ISBN-13: 978-0-7377-4571-9
ISBN-10: 0-7377-4571-1

3 1561 00232 8957

Printed in the United States of America
1 2 3 4 5 6 7 13 12 11 10 09

Printed by Bang Printing, Brainerd, MN, 1st Ptg., 12/2009

Contents

Chapter 1

The Crying Woman

I n the foothills of Colorado, several streams join to become the headwaters of the mighty Rio Grande. On its journey to the Gulf of Mexico, this majestic river carves a natural border between Texas on the north and Mexico on the south. Along the way it brings life-giving water to farms and towns. For an unfortunate few who find themselves alone near the river at night, it may bring terror and even death. According to legend, the banks of the Rio Grande and other waterways of the American Southwest and Latin America are the domain of the vengeful spirit, La Llorona (la-yor-oh-nah), the Crying Woman.

Some people claim the spirit appears as a beautiful woman draped in a flowing white burial robe.

According to legend, the banks of the Rio Grande are haunted by La Llorona, the Crying Woman.

Others say she is an old hag dressed in black. Her long black hair hides a skeletal face with empty eye sockets. Her razor-sharp fingernails gleam like polished metal, ready to claw out the eyes of a victim. Believers agree that she roams riverbanks and lakeshores in search of prey, usually children. Once she has a victim in her grip, she drags him or her to a

A Sorrowful Goddess

Cihuacoatl (snake woman) is the Aztec goddess of women who die in childbirth. She wears a feather headdress and white robe, her face painted half red and half black. She is believed to roam at night, stealing children to use as soldiers. Her sorrowful cry is carried on the night wind. "Oh hijos mios" (Oh my children), she sobs, "ya ha llegado vuestra destruccion" (your destruction has arrived).

horrible death in the water. The last thing the ill-fated person may see is the dark blood oozing from the spirit's vacant eyes.

From the Mists of Time

The tale of La Llorona is different from one region to another. Most of the stories, however, have one thing in common. The Crying Woman is the tragic ghost of a mother who drowned her children then took her own life. Her punishment for murder and suicide is to wander the earth for eternity, searching for her children. Some historians trace the roots of the legend to the **massacre** of the Aztec people by Spanish soldiers in the 16th century.

La Malinche, the Mexican companion of Hernan Cortes, who killed her young sons after being visited by a spirt.

1892

Copyright C.E.Wright

DONA MARINA, INTERPRETER OF CORTES.

In the early 1500s, Mayan traders purchased a young Aztec girl as a slave from her own parents. The girl had a talent for language and soon learned to speak the tongue of her captors. When soldiers arrived from Spain, the girl learned Spanish. Known as La Malinche, she became the companion of the Spanish leader, Hernán Cortés, and gave birth to twin boys. She told Cortés about an ambush that her people had planned. Because of her help, he survived, but thousands of Aztecs were killed.

At first Cortés decided to remain in the new land against the wishes of the king and queen of Spain. In 1522 they sent a beautiful woman to tempt him to return to Europe. Not only did Cortés agree, but he also planned to take the twin boys with him, leaving La Malinche behind. La Malinche realized that she had made a terrible mistake by trusting Cortés and having his children. As she cried about her fate, a spirit appeared and told her that if her boys went to Spain, one of them would return and destroy her people.

As horrible as the choice was, La Malinche made up her mind to sacrifice her own children to save her people. She gathered up the two little boys and dashed to a nearby lake with soldiers in pursuit. Before the Spaniards could stop her, she stabbed each child through the heart. As their lifeless bodies fell into the water, she dropped to her knees and began to sob. Descending into madness, she remained on the shoreline for the rest of her life, crying for the loss of her sons. She never knew that she also failed to save her people. Years later Hernán Cortés wrote in a letter that the defeat of the Aztec Empire of Mexico would not have been possible without the help of La Malinche. In Mexico the word *malinche* has come to mean betrayal.

Some historians disagree with the **traditional** story of La Malinche. They claim she had only one son, Don Martín Cortés, who lived to adulthood. They also say she married a Spaniard and possibly had a daughter.

Tears from Other Lands

The story of La Malinche is similar to stories in other cultures. One of the most well-known is the ancient Greek myth of Medea the **sorceress**. Medea fell in love with the Greek hero, Jason, and used magic to

A Terrible Choice

When the Spanish arrived in Mexico in 1519, they were amazed by the beauty of the Indian children. Soldiers took the most attractive children and gave them to their wives. Some of the Indian women killed their young in order to keep the Spaniards from taking them.

The legend of Greek goddess Medea and her lover Jason is similar to La Llorona in that she killed their two sons after discovering his affair with a new woman.

help him steal a golden **fleece** from her own father. Jason and Medea had two sons, but their love did not last. Jason abandoned Medea for a new love, a princess of Corinth. In her rage, Medea sent a poisoned robe to Jason's new bride, killed the two sons, and escaped in a chariot drawn by dragons. Unlike La Malinche, Medea was not sorry at all for what she had done.

In the Philippines, there is a legend of a mermaid known as the Weeping Woman. The mermaid had many children. At the age of fourteen, each child was allowed to decide whether or not to become human. When her favorite son chose to be human, the mermaid was unhappy, but accepted his decision. Not long after, a fisherman accidentally killed her son. The mermaid angrily swore to get revenge on all humans. Today **superstitious** people blame the Weeping Woman whenever a child drowns.

In Chile, La Pucullén is an **omen** of death. Like La Llorona, the crying woman of Chile searches through the night for her baby son who died in her arms. It is said that dogs howl when she is close by. Although she can be dangerous, La Pucullén may show some mercy. She cries for people who have died, and a pool of her tears marks the spot in the cemetery where the **deceased** should be buried. The dead can safely reach the **afterlife** by following her footprints. Although her cries may be heard by anyone at night, La Pucullén can only be seen by a person who is about to die. In some tales, a person who wants to see her must rub a dog's tears in his or her eyes.

Ghostly Beginnings and Encounters

The earliest recorded sightings of La Llorona began in Mexico City in the middle of the 16th century. Terrified peasants swore that the spirit drifted through the central plaza of the city under the light of a full moon. Her visits were often followed by drownings, so La Llorona became an omen of death.

Not all believers think that La Llorona's story began in the 16th century. Throughout the Americas, there are more modern versions of the origin of the frightful ghost. One such tale is of a young Mexican woman named Maria. Known for her great beauty, Maria fell in love with a rich man and hoped to become his wife. His family would

The earliest recorded sightings of La Llorona began in Mexico City when peasants swore that the spirit drifted through the central plaza of the city under the light of a full moon.

The Crying Woman of Panama

In Panama the crying woman is called La Tulivieja. She is said to be a hideous woman with holes in her face, chicken feet, and long straggly hair. To this day, people who live near lakes and rivers claim to have heard La Tulivieja's chilling wail.

not accept Maria, so they did not marry. But he claimed he loved her, and they had three children together.

At first the man visited often. As time passed, his visits were less frequent. When he did visit, he brought gifts for his children but ignored Maria. One day when she was at the market, Maria saw the man she loved riding in a carriage with a wealthy young woman.

The next time he came to see his children, Maria demanded an explanation. He admitted that he planned to marry the other woman. In a fury, Maria dragged their children to the banks of the Rio Grande and drowned them. As their small bodies sank in the icy water, she realized what she had done. Under a full moon, she threw herself off a cliff. The villagers found her body and buried her, but Maria does not rest. Local people claim that she rises from her grave to walk at night, crying for her murdered children.

The Wandering Spirit

In another version of La Llorona's story, Maria is a beautiful single mother. Rather than stay home to care for her children, she goes out night after night to dance and enjoy the attention of young men. When the neighbors realize that Maria is neglecting her children, they criticize her. Outraged, she blames her children. Some storytellers say that the children drowned in a flood while Maria was off dancing. Others say she drowned them herself in a fit of fury. The result is the same. Maria realizes that she has lost the only people who truly loved her. Not wanting to live without them, she kills herself. When she arrives at the gates of heaven, she learns that she cannot enter without her children. Maria returns to Earth as a lonely spirit, searching for her children.

In parts of Texas and in Kansas City, Missouri, the story takes a slightly different turn. As in other tales, the young mother is beautiful and attracts the attention of a rich man, but she loves her two children. Her duty as their mother is more important to her than a relationship with the rich man. At first she resists the man, but at last she falls in love with him. The man claims that he loves her too, but he will not marry her because he does not want a fam-

Another version of La Llorona's story entails a mother who neglected her children by leaving them home so she could go dancing in the streets of the village at night.

ily. The heartbreak drives the young mother to the brink of madness. At last she decides that her children are in the way. One night she takes them to a bridge over a river, stabs them both, and lets their small bodies topple into the water. In a **frenzy**, she runs to the home of her love to tell him what she has done so that they can be together. When he opens the door and sees her gown soaked with blood, he screams at her to get away from him and slams the door.

Then the woman comes to her senses and races back to the river to save her children, but it is too late. The water has carried their bodies away. Throwing herself into the river, the woman drowns, but her spirit is cursed to wander the banks

A Rare Illness

A few new mothers suffer from an uncommon mental and emotional illness called postpartum psychosis. In extreme cases the symptoms may include hearing voices or seeing things that are not really there. It can lead to a new mother doing harm to herself or her child. The sufferer may feel angry or guilty because of her thoughts. In very rare cases, a woman may feel that someone or something is commanding her to kill her child.

forever, crying for her young ones. Unlike other stories, God punishes this La Llorona for her crime by making her head look like the head of a horse.

A Dangerous Phantom

In the United States, La Llorona encounters have been reported from California to Illinois, from Colorado to the Mexican border, and as far north as Oregon and the banks of the Yellowstone River in Montana. The spirit cries in Spanish, "¿Donde estan mis hijos?" (Where are my children?), or "¿Has visto a mis hijos?" (Have you seen my children?). People who stop to help her or speak to her may be in terrible danger. It is said that the crying woman kills without mercy, and a child who wanders too close to the water is an easy target. She is also thought to prey upon men who are out late drinking instead of being at home with their families. She may spare the life of a man, but coming face-to-face with her leaves the victim completely insane.

The sightings are usually near freshwater, such as a river, pond, or lake, but in California, there are stories of La Llorona sightings on beaches along the Pacific Ocean. In many California cities, riverbeds have been lined in concrete and are used as flood control channels. Believers claim that the spirit haunts those channels or the bridges above them. Even water tanks and reservoirs may harbor the evil spirit.

Santa Fe, New Mexico, has its share of La Llo-

Tales of the ghostly La Llorona are spread all over the United States, though several center around the Sante Fe River.

rona hauntings. In an office building near the Santa Fe River, some people who work in the building insist that they have heard wailing in what appears to be an empty hallway. The building is located on land that was once a Spanish-Indian graveyard.

One resident of Santa Fe recalls hearing La Llorona when he was a little boy. He was home alone when he heard what he thought were the mournful cries of an animal. He ran outside to shoo the creature away. There was something nearby, but it was not an animal. It was a presence that seemed old, and the boy was terrified. Today he believes that the cries he heard were those of a ghostly woman mourning for the dead.

Strange Sightings

Perhaps the most unexpected sightings are those reported in the neighborhood of Cudahee in Gary, Indiana. Many years ago, Mexicans **immigrated** to Gary to work in the steel mills. It is likely that the legend of La Llorona traveled with them. Workers leaving the mills at night say that sometimes a crying woman can be seen just over the bridge, near the corner of Fifth and Cline avenues. The story may have started with the death of several children in an auto accident in the 1930s. The mother of the children eventually died of her grief. According to the legend, the poor woman continues to return to the spot, crying out for her family.

Many of the traditional stories of La Llorona take place near the Rio Grande. It is no surprise that there are still sightings of the spirit along the river. The spirit is usually seen or heard in the bosque, a 200-mile (322km) strip of trees and other vegeta-

In 1948 two families were sitting around a campfire in Texas when two of their children were held in a trance by a strange woman on the riverbank.

tion that lines the banks of the Rio Grande from New Mexico to Texas.

In 1948 in Socorro, Texas, two families went camping. They pitched their tents in the shade of cottonwood trees near enough to the Rio Grande to enjoy the breezes. On the second evening of their stay, the parents chatted while their children played near the water. When the sounds of the children playing faded, the parents called for them, but only two returned, frightened and breathless. They declared that the other youngsters, a boy and his sister, were talking to a woman on the riverbank. The adults raced to the spot and saw a woman standing in the shadows. She was reaching for the children, who looked as if they were in a **trance**. The shouts of their parents broke the spell, and the children ran away from the woman. Both families piled into the car and raced away without looking back.

In the 1980s another sighting took place in the same area. Several men from Socorro were enjoying an evening on the riverbank. They were sharing stories around a campfire when the wind picked up. All at once a cry rose near the river. A blood-curdling scream followed, then another and another. Something was moving through the dark woods, coming closer and closer to the men. The horrified men did not know where to run. Then the cries stopped. The men left the riverbank in a hurry and never returned to that part of the river.

Many inhabitants of the small town of Pilar, New Mexico, claim that the cries of La Llorona are

Beware of Hitchhikers

The town of East Bernard, Texas, was established around 1850. The first homes were built on the eastern bank of the San Bernard River. Eventually the San Bernard Bridge was built to connect the east and west banks. According to local folklore, drivers should never stop to pick up a lone woman on the bridge, because it might be La Llorona herself.

common in the area. Those who find themselves in the bosque at night quickly head for the safety of home when the wailing begins.

Crybaby Bridges

In parts of the United States, La Llorona's story is sometimes connected to another urban legend. An urban legend is a scary rumor, or tale, that is passed by word-of-mouth. The person telling it often claims to have actually experienced the frighten-

ing event or to know someone who did. One such legend is about crybaby bridges. The name is given to any bridge haunted by the ghost of a drowned child. The state of Ohio is known to have at least 24 crybaby bridges, including those at Rogue's Hollow, Egypt Road, Helltown, and the Screaming Bridge at Maud Hughes Road. In many cases, witnesses who claim to have heard the cries of a ghost child also report seeing a woman in white on the riverbank or on the bridge. Some warn that the woman is La Llorona. They believe that a drowning death draws her to the site, where she searches for more victims.

The story of La Llorona is often told as a warning. Boys and girls are cautioned that if they go near the river after dark, they might become victims of the spirit.

Crybaby bridges throughout the United States are supposedly haunted by the ghost of a drowned child.

27

Mothers tell their teenage girls about how La Llorona was betrayed by a man, so they should choose their mates wisely. Teenage boys are warned that La Llorona is an angry ghost that holds a **grudge** against men. In some cultures La Llorona is a **symbol** of the **consequences** that unfold when women fail to love and protect their children.

La Llorona in Modern Culture

To most people, La Llorona is a tragic and fearsome ghost. But some researchers have a new view of her. They think that the legend is a symbol of a woman's resistance to male control in the family and in society. In spite of the horror of her story, La Llorona made her own decisions and acted on them. She was not willing to be quiet and do what society said she had to do. The researchers see her as a powerful figure.

This new image of the Crying Woman as a symbol of **defiance** has begun to appear in a wide range of ways. In June 2004, artist Juana Alicia completed a mural titled, *La Llorona's Sacred Waters.* The beautiful work covers the walls of a building at the corner of York and 24th streets in San Francisco. La Llorona is the central figure in the mural, which depicts women of Bolivia and India fighting for environmental and social issues. This is one of many works of art that has spread the legend of La Llorona far beyond its original borders.

La Llorona has been part of Latin American culture for centuries. Today the Crying Woman is the subject of books, paintings, films, plays, music, and pop culture. In 2002 La Llorona appeared in a commercial for the California Milk Processor Board in which she is crying not for her children, but for milk. Her image is used to promote products from coffee to underwear. For example, the Artisan Chili Oil Company in Fresno, California, makes a line of spicy salsas called Salsas La Llorona. It is even possible to purchase bumper stickers that read, "Honk if you've seen La Llorona."

Haunting Pages

La Llorona also appears in print. *Woman Hollering Creek and Other Stories*, published in 1991, is a collection of short stories written by Sandra Cisneros. The stories refer to several figures that are symbolic of Mexican American women, including La Malinche and La Llorona. Although there are many books that tell the traditional story of La Llorona, Cisneros's work stands out because she transforms the spirit from an evil being to something more heroic. The main character learns to accept La Llo-

Sandra Cisneros is one of several authors who wrote stories about La Llorona.

rona's cries as a joyous holler rather than a mournful wail.

The first issue of the comic book series, Love and Rockets, was published in 1981. The series was created by Gilbert and Jaime Hernandez for older teen readers. The seventh issue, *The Death of Speedy*, introduces a punk rock group called La Llorona. Although many Mexican American teens already knew the story of the weeping ghost, the comic book made her a part of American pop culture.

From Myth to Canvas

In the late 20th century, La Llorona was a familiar subject for many Latin American artists. Santa Barraza painted portraits of both La Malinche and La Llorona in the 1990s.

Victor Zubeldia created a collection of forty images of La Llorona. Each haunting image is a unique vision. Perhaps the most frightening is an oil painting titled, Breeding Crows that shows the mournful spirit with bleeding eyes. Pictures of the collection are included in the book, La Llorona, the Wailing Woman, published in 2003.

On Film and Television

La Llorona is a character in several horror films. The classic black-and-white, Spanish-language film, *The Crying Woman* was released in 1933. It stars Virginia Zuri as La Llorona. The story takes place in modern Mexico and features a family with a young

A Tragic Setting

The Cry **is a horror movie that was filmed in 2007 in New York City and New Mexico. When director, Bernadine Santistevan, chose a site near Pilar, New Mexico for a scene in which La Llorona drowns her child, she did not know that a tragedy had already taken place there. Before shooting, the director learned that in 2002, a woman named Bernadine Flores drowned her two young children in that area of the Rio Grande. Flores took her own life immediately afterward. Santistevan decided to go ahead and film at the site.**

son. The family does not realize that they are being watched by a strange, cloaked figure. Eventually, the cloaked figure kidnaps the boy and attempts to sacrifice him. The origin of La Llorona is told in flashbacks.

Perhaps the best known of the horror classics, *La Maldición de La Llorona*, was released in Mexico in 1963. It was released with English subtitles in the United States in 1969 under the name, *Curse of the Crying Woman*. The film stars Rosa Arenas. Fans of the movie praise the eerie setting and shadowy

The legend of La Llorona has made it to the big screen as well in films such as the horror classic, *Curse of the Crying Woman* (1963).

photography. Arenas plays a young woman named Amelia who goes to stay with her Aunt Selma in an old mansion. The story includes mysterious murders, family secrets, and an unusual corpse in the family crypt.

In the wildly popular Harry Potter films in the United States, actress Shirley Henderson plays Moaning Myrtle, a wailing ghost similar to La Llorona. Myrtle haunts the second floor girls' bathroom at Hogwarts School. In the tradition of the Crying Woman, Myrtle is most often found near water in a sink, bathtub, or some part of the plumbing. Myrtle moans, whines, sobs, and cries to anyone who is willing to listen, and many who would rather not.

Fans of the popular television show, *Supernatural*, may have seen a representation of La Llorona in the 2005 pilot for the show. The series follows two brothers who track, fight, and eliminate monsters, vampires, ghosts, and **demons**. In the pilot, the two search for their father, who was last heard from in the town of Jericho where men have been disappearing. The culprit turns out to be a woman in white, much like a modern version of La Llorona.

The Spirit in the Music

La Llorona is also in music. There are several versions of a folk song about La Llorona. One of the most popular includes **lyrics** based in part on a poem by Luis Martz. In fact, a version of that song is included on the soundtrack of the Academy

Lila Downs, a breakthrough artist in Mexican music, wrote and performed the song "La Llorona" for the *Frida* soundtrack.

Award–winning film, *Little Miss Sunshine* (2006).

Many folk singers have recorded "La Llorona." Chavela Vargas rose to fame in Mexico during the 1950s and 1960s. In 2003 she returned to perform the song at New York's Carnegie Hall at the age of 83. She also performed the song for the 2002 film, *Frida*, about Mexican artist Frida Kahlo.

Mexican American singer Lhasa de Sela's first album is titled *La Llorona*. It was released in 1997 and includes a blend of original and traditional songs. *La Llorona* was a major hit.

Lila Downs has been called one of the freshest and most original voices in Mexican music. She wrote and performed several songs for the film *Frida*. The soundtrack includes the songs "La Llorona" and "Burn it Blue," which Downs performed at the Academy Awards ceremony in 2003.

On Stage

The tragedy of the Crying Woman is a perfect subject for the drama of opera. *La Llorona* is the title of an opera in three acts. The **libretto** and original story are by **Chicano** author, Rudolfo Anaya, and the music was composed by Daniel Steven Crafts. The opera begins in a modern family home on Halloween night. A mom and her young son, who is dressed as a goblin, are baking cookies. When the grandfather arrives, he tells the little boy to be careful because La Llorona is roaming in the dark outside. When the little boy asks who that is, his grandfather begins the tale of La Malinche. The stage grows dark as the scene changes. A magnificent Aztec temple appears on the stage and the story unfolds.

A very different tale of misfortune is told in the play, *La Llorona, Weeping Women of Echo Park*, first directed by Henriëtte Brouwers. It is a collection of stories about immigrant women who cried because they had to leave their children behind when they came to the United States. The first to speak is La Malinche, who tells the audience that the women are slaves like her. Some of the women were modern-day slaves, victims of **human trafficking**. Others entered the United States illegally. When they are caught in immigration raids, they are deported and must often leave their American-born children behind. Like La Llorona, they cry for their lost children. *La Llorona, Weeping Women of*

Best Before Dark

La Llorona Park is a lovely family area located along the Rio Grande in Las Cruces, New Mexico. The park has a playground, picnic benches, and hiking trails. Some residents, however, say that it is best to leave the park before dark.

Chicano author Rudolfo Anaya wrote the dramatic three-act opera *La Llorona*.

Echo Park is the third production in a series of plays that include *La Llorona, Weeping Women and War*, and *La Llorona, Weeping Women on Skid Row*.

The tale of La Llorona began as an oral tradition. Over the past century, her story has spread throughout different cultures in a variety of ways, from literature and art to films and music. She has come to represent the social position of modern women and the two parts of Mexican and Mexican American identity. She is a victim, a hero, a pop icon, and a symbol of traditional culture in a new and changing world.

Still, no matter how society changes, there will always be those who gather around a campfire to hear a creepy tale. There will always be those who feel a chill and perhaps a thrill when an eerie, distant cry drifts on an evening breeze, or when a filmy form materializes from the shadows. For them, La Llorona will always be a vengeful spirit, a terrifying phantom, and a reason to stay far away from the river late at night.

Glossary

afterlife: An existence believed to go on after death.

Chicano: A North American male of Mexican descent.

consequences: The result or outcome of an act or behavior.

deceased: A person who has died.

defiance: Refusal to obey, rebelliousness.

demons: Evil spirits.

fleece: The wool of sheep.

frenzy: Uncontrolled excitement or agitation.

grudge: A long-lasting feeling of ill will.

human trafficking: The sale or transport of human beings who are forced to work.

immigrated: Moved to a new place or country.

libretto: The words of an opera.

lyrics: The words of a song.

massacre: The killing of large numbers of people or animals.

omen: A sign of something that will happen in the future.

postpartum psychosis: A mental disorder often accompanied by an inability to determine reality suffered by women after they give birth.

sorceress: A woman thought to have magical powers.

superstitious: Believing in omens or rituals performed to bring good or bad luck.

symbol: Something that represents an idea or concept.

traditional: Normal or customary based on common practice.

trance: A daze or hypnotic state.

For Further Exploration

Books

Gloria E. Anzaldua, *Prietita and the Ghost Woman.* San Francisco, CA: Children's Book Press, 2001. This is a bilingual picture book about a girl who gets lost in the woods and meets La Llorona. The ending is not what the reader might expect.

Joe Hayes, *The Day It Snowed Tortillas: El Día Que Nevaron Tortillas.* El Paso, TX: Cinco Puntos Press, 2003. This book offers a collection of folktales in Spanish and English for middle-grade readers. Some tales are funny. Others are clever. The tale of La Llorona is traditional and creepy.

———, *La Llorona: The Weeping Woman.* El Paso, TX: Cinco Puntos Press, 2006. This bilingual picture book tells the classic ghost story of La Llorona.

Linda Lowry and Richard Keep, *The Tale of La Llorona: A Mexican Folktale.* Minneapolis, MN: First Avenue Editions, 2008. This book offers a retelling of the La Llorona folktale. It is written for lower reading levels.

Web sites

The Cry. http://www.lallorona.com/. This is the website for the film *The Cry*. It includes a timeline of the La Llorona legend, information about similar legends, and details about the making of the film.

Legends of America. http://www.legendsofamerica.com/HC-WeepingWoman1.html. This site includes overviews of many American legends, ghostly stories, tales of treasure, and legends of the Old West. There is a section on American history and tips for traveling around the nation. The section on La Llorona includes stories from people who claim to have encountered the spirit.

Index

45

Picture Credits

About the Author

Q. L. Pearce has written more than 100 books for children and more than 30 classroom workbooks and teacher manuals on the topics of reading, science, math, and values. She also writes science-related articles for magazines; regularly gives presentations at schools, bookstores, and libraries; and is a frequent contributor to the educational program of the Los Angeles County Fair. Pearce is the assistant regional advisor for the Society of Children's Book Writers and Illustrators.